HANDBOOKS OF EUROPEAN NATIONAL DANCES

EDITED BY
VIOLET ALFORD

DANCES OF ENGLAND & WALES

Plate 1
Morris men from Bampton, Oxon., and Ruardean, Forest of Dean

DANCES OF ENGLAND & WALES

MAUD KARPELES
and
LOÏS BLAKE

PUBLISHED
UNDER THE AUSPICES OF
THE ROYAL ACADEMY OF DANCING
AND THE
LING PHYSICAL EDUCATION ASSOCIATION

LONDON
MAX PARRISH & COMPANY

ILLUSTRATED BY
ROWLAND A. BEARD
ASSISTANT EDITOR
YVONNE MOYSE

First published in 1950

This edition published in 2021 by
The Noverre Press
Southwold House
Isington Road
Binsted
Hampshire
GU34 4PH

ISBN 978-1-914311-01-7

© 2021 The Noverre Press

CONTENTS

DANCES OF ENGLAND	*Page* 7
The Sword Dance	9
The Morris Dance	10
Processional Dances	13
The Country Dance	14
Music	15
Costume	16
Where Dancing May Be Seen	17
DANCES OF WALES	18
Seasonal Customs	18
Country Dances	19
Music	19
Costume	20
Where Dancing May Be Seen	20
THE DANCES	21
Poise of the Body and Holds	22
Basic Steps	22
Speed the Plough	23
Circassian Circle	26
Lads a Bunchum	28
Rhif Wyth	35
BIBLIOGRAPHY	38

Illustrations in Colour, pages 2, 12, 29, 39
Map of England and Wales, page 6

DANCES OF ENGLAND

BY MAUD KARPELES

Thanks to Cecil Sharp, England can take its place among the nations in the galaxy of folk music and dance that is presented in this series of European handbooks. The natural flow of folk dance, like that of all other traditional arts, tends to become choked with the rise of industrialism; and this has been particularly noticeable in England, where during the nineteenth century we allowed our native music and dances to be reduced to an underground trickle. But for their timely salvage by Cecil Sharp at the beginning of the century and the revival which he subsequently initiated, they would probably by now have vanished past recall. Encouraged by the interest which he aroused, age-old traditions which had lingered on in the remote byways have acquired a new lease of life.

Indeed, a visitor from overseas wandering through the quiet lanes and villages of England might come upon scenes which would make him wonder whether he had not slipped back into a past age or been transported to some far-off country. If he were in the neighbourhood of the Staffordshire village of Abbots Bromley on a morning early in September, he might see emerging from the mists of dawn a procession of curious figures, half human, half animal. As the procession approached he would distinguish a company of six men, each bearing the huge antlers of a reindeer, together with other curiously garbed persons. The strains of a concertina would fall on his ear and he would be the witness of a solemn ceremonial dance in which the dancers move in serpentine patterns, alternating with a challenging forward and backward motion by two confronting lines of antler-bearers. Just as mysteriously as the procession had appeared it would vanish round the bend of the road.

Enquiries would evoke the information that the dancers were men of the village and that the horns, except for that one day in the year, were safeguarded in the parish church.

Or, if the season were spring-time and our overseas visitor were staying in the Cornish fishing village of Padstow, he would be awakened late on May Eve by the sound of men singing in chorus a song which, in its freshness and gaiety, would remind him that 'Sumer is icumen in'. And rising the next morning and strolling through the village he would see coming towards him, perhaps along a leafy lane, a weird-looking monster with its attendants who might have been transported straight from the Fiji Islands. This would be the Hobby Horse, a hoop-shaped contraption of black tar-painted canvas, a small horse's head with snapping jaws in front; the round object surmounted by a high conical hat and garishly painted mask. The rider is completely hidden from view inside the 'horse' which, with an attendant, heavily gambols and dances throughout the day to the accompaniment of song and music. The streets are thronged with gay crowds, who express amusement or simulate fear as the Hobby Horse makes a sudden dart in an endeavour to catch a woman beneath his black hangings.

The Whitsuntide Morris Dance, familiar to Shakespeare, was another ceremony which at one time took place in most of the villages lying in the heart of England. Today only the Oxfordshire village of Bampton-in-the-Bush has maintained the tradition unbroken, but there every Whit-Monday the dancers are to be seen, gaily decorated with ribbons and flowers, dancing with unconscious grace to the lively accompaniment of a blind fiddler.

Cecil Sharp was not always fortunate enough to see the dances performed by a complete team. In fact, more often than not he had to get his information from single individuals—the only survivors who remembered the dance—and much patience and skill were needed to gather together the fine corpus of dance tradition which we now possess.

This dance tradition can be divided into two categories: firstly those of a ritual or ceremonial character usually danced on prescribed occasions and by picked dancers; and secondly the Country dances, performed on all occasions when people meet together for recreation.

The two main types of ritual dances are the Sword and the Morris dances which, though possibly related in origin, are very different in character. Both are danced by men only.

THE SWORD DANCE

The Sword dances, not to be confused with the Scottish Sword dances, are traditionally performed in the midwinter season. They are found now in the North-East of England, and are danced in ring formation by five, six or eight men, each of whom carries a sword in one hand and holds the point of his neighbour's sword in the other. Thus bound in a ring of steel (sometimes wooden laths are substituted for the swords), they perform intricate evolutions, passing under the swords, jumping over them, turning the ring inside out, and so on. The climax of the dance is brought about by the swords being meshed together in a star-shaped design called the Lock. This symbol is then held aloft by the leader and usually placed round the neck of a 'victim' who kneels or stands in the centre of the ring. At a given word from the leader the dancers draw their swords and the victim suffers a mimic decapitation and death. In addition to this dramatic episode there is often a suggestion of drama in the characters accompanying the dancers, such as a Man-woman, a Clown and others, and also in the 'calling-on' song in which the singer, after introducing the several dancers, makes the apparently irrelevant announcement that he is going to kill a bullock.

From the hints given in these songs and from the tense emotion inherent in the dance we should suspect that it had some serious underlying purpose and that it was the survival of some bygone ritual. This supposition is borne out by a Play of which the dance was once an integral part. Several versions and fragments of this Play have been noted. It is a curious hotchpotch, showing the influence of the Mummers' Play and containing elements of debased literary composition. Most of it consists of unintelligible clowning, yet it grips the imagination. The Play centres round the killing of a victim and his subsequent resurrection by a comic doctor who enters the arena riding his human horse.

One cannot give a precise meaning to these mummeries or to the other dance ceremonies that are to be found in our countryside, but we may be justified in supposing that they are forms of fertility rite, and that the death and resurrection theme of the Sword dance is symbolic of the cyclic sequence of the seasons. Dancers and players are practising mimetic magic, in which the thing that is desired—in this case the awakening of spring after the sleep of winter—must be enacted to bring it about.

Nowadays the Sword dance, or dances, for there are many different forms (including some which are danced with short strips of steel called rappers), are usually performed by miners. The dance is not peculiar to England, but is known in many countries in Europe.*

THE MORRIS DANCE

Morris Dance is a generic term used by the folk rather indiscriminately for various types of dances, for the Mummers' Play and even for the Sword dance. We are, however, accustomed to associate it particularly with a certain type of dance which is now performed in the Midland counties of England.

Cecil Sharp discovered many forms of Morris dances in Oxfordshire, Gloucestershire, Warwickshire and Northamp-

* Cf. *Dances of Czechoslovakia*, *Dances of Austria* and other books in this series.

tonshire. It is danced by six men, sometimes accompanied by a Fool, a Clown and other characters. The costume of the dancers varies in different villages, but it is always profusely decorated with gaily coloured ribbons in the form of rosettes, streamers and so on; when hats are worn these are also decorated with ribbons and flowers. An old countrywoman once told Cecil Sharp: 'It takes twelve yards of ribbon to dress a Morris dancer.' The dancers wear pads of little bells strapped on to the shin of each leg, and the step is designed to effect a rhythmical jingling of the bells. A white handkerchief is carried in each hand, or else a wooden stick in one or both hands. The waving and fluttering of the handkerchiefs is an integral part of the dance movement, as is the rhythmical clashing of sticks in the stick dances.

The many interesting customs associated with the Morris dance seem to show that the Morris, like the Sword dance, had its origin in fertility rites. There were processions in which a live lamb was decorated, paraded through the village and afterwards killed, cooked and eaten at a feast; there were deer hunts and other indications of animal sacrifice. At Bampton, dancers are accompanied by a man bearing a flower-decorated sword impaling a cake, which is said to have magic properties. A young girl placing a piece of the cake under her pillow at night will dream of her sweetheart.

As with the Sword dance, it is difficult to give a precise explanation of the meaning and origin of the Morris dance. The ringing of the bells combined with the patter of the feet may be intended to wake up the earth spirit; or the high leaps to which Shakespeare draws attention—'I saw him caper upright like a wild Morisco'—may be mimetic magic to encourage the crops to spring up and grow tall. Again, the ringing of the bells, the waving of the handkerchiefs and the beating of the sticks may be to frighten away evil spirits, or the clashing of sticks may represent some sort

Plate 2
Sword dancer from
Earsdon, Northumbria

of fight, possibly between the forces of light and darkness.

The term Morris has been the subject of much debate. Its obvious derivation from Moorish has led people to suppose that the dance is of Moorish origin. The dance is, however, too widely distributed throughout Europe for this to be the case. There are various explanations of the term, but the most probable is that the dance was called Moorish or Morisco, not because the dancers *were* Moors, but because they looked like Moors on account of blackening their faces. This they did as a form of disguise—always an important element in a ritual dance, in which the dancers act in an official and not in a personal capacity. The smudge of black which the Morris dancer to this day sometimes puts on his cheek 'so that no one shan't know you' is evidence of the persistence of tradition.

Another possible theory is that the dance was called Moorish as being synonymous with pagan, that is an Infidel.*

Certainly the dance is imbued with magic. In our country its significance has been largely forgotten, although there is still a vague feeling that it brings 'luck'; but among less sophisticated people, such as the Balkan peasants, dances akin to our Morris dances are performed as a means of curing the sick, and mothers will lay their children on the ground for the dancers to step and caper over them.

In both the Morris and the Sword dance the members of the traditional team are carefully picked and subjected to vigorous training.

PROCESSIONAL DANCES

There are many Processional dances which are performed on certain days of the year. Some, like the Horn dance already mentioned, are performed by a prescribed number of

* See Rodney Gallop: 'The Origins of the Morris Dance.' *Journal of the E.F.D.S.S.*, 1934.

dancers and by men only. In others, particularly the May Day dances, such as the well-known Cornish Helston Furry dance, the whole village takes part, dancing not only through the streets but in and out of the houses. At Helston, and at Castleton in Derbyshire, the dancers used in days gone by to carry freshly cut green boughs and flowers. In most cases it is customary to stop occasionally and perform a stationary dance. One is inclined to think that these Processionals are the remains of a seasonal lustration round the village with halts at certain sacred spots for the performance of a special ceremony.

THE COUNTRY DANCE

It is probable that our Country dances, now purely social, have their origin in the May Day dances. There are many forms of Country dance: Longways 'for as many as will' or for a limited number of couples, Rounds for a varying number of couples, Squares for four couples, and other forms. It is generally supposed that the Longways type, in which the men and women dance opposite each other (as in Speed the Plough), is a development of the Processional dance, whilst the Rounds and Squares, in which the men and women dance side by side, are descended from the old Rounds, of which the Maypole dance is a prototype; and here it must be said that the plaiting of ribbons, dearly loved by schoolteachers and children, is not an English tradition. The old English Maypole, which symbolised the living tree, was an object of reverence. It was decorated, not with long ribbons, but with greenery and on its summit there was usually a garland of leaves and flowers. The Circassian Circle is the kind of dance that was once performed round the Maypole.

Unlike the Morris and Sword, which so far as we know were danced only by the 'folk', the Country dance was popular with all classes of society. It was danced at Court, not only in England but on the Continent, and we were known in Tudor days as 'the dancing English', renowned for carrying a 'fair presence'. In the middle of the seventeenth century John Playford, the music publisher, edited and published many of our Country dances under the title of *The English Dancing Master*—changed to *The Dancing Master* in later editions. At that period the Country dance was at its prime, and although the majority of the dances in the Playford collections are not pure folk dances they may be said to have a folk basis. The Country dance ordinarily consisted of a series of figures arbitrarily chosen to fit a given tune; only in certain instances did a particular combination of figures become stereotyped and achieve universal acceptance. Though the older dances in the Playford collections had probably been danced for many generations in the same way to the same tune, others are the product of the conscious manipulation of traditional material by dancing-masters and editors.

During the eighteenth and nineteenth centuries the Longways dances achieved popularity and most of the dances which are now traditionally performed are of this type.

Undue emphasis has, perhaps, been laid on the somewhat hypothetical origin of the dances, but it would be an entire misrepresentation to regard our dances merely as relics of the past—the shells of beliefs that have been outgrown and forgotten. They have a living beauty and as an expression of those unchanging emotions which we share with our ancestors they belong as much to this generation as to the past. This fundamental quality of the dances was well expressed by a famous Morris dancer who said, 'Our dances are now what they were and what they will always be'.

MUSIC

Except in children's games, singing practically never accompanies the dances, although song tunes are often adopted as instrumental dance airs.

The traditional accompaniment for the Morris dance is the pipe and tabor, often known as whittle and dub, a combination of two instruments played by one man. The pipe is a short wooden three-holed instrument which the player holds in his left hand, using his thumb and first two fingers to cover the holes. An octave and two notes can easily be produced from the pipe; a clever player can achieve a considerably wider compass. The tabor, a small drum, is suspended by a strap over the left wrist and is beaten by a stick held in the right hand. Nowadays the pipe and tabor have been superseded by the fiddle or concertina, and these are the instruments most generally used for other forms of English folk dancing.

There is also an English form of bagpipe, commonly called the Northumbrian Small-pipes, which is still played in the North of England, although no longer as a dance accompaniment. The Small-pipes differ considerably from the better known Scottish pipes. The tone is smaller but sweeter and is more suited for indoor performance than that of the Scottish pipes. As in the Irish *uilleann* (elbow) bagpipe, the wind is supplied not by the breath of the player but by small bellows placed under one arm.

COSTUME

There is no traditional dress for Country dancing. These, being social dances, are and always were danced in the costume of the period. Unlike most European countries, England cannot boast of distinctive regional costumes, although the patterns of women's sunbonnets and of farmworkers' smocks vary from district to district.

The special dress of the Morris and Sword dance teams varies from village to village.

WHERE DANCING MAY BE SEEN
PERFORMED BY TRADITIONAL DANCERS

Sword Dances. Short sword or rapper dances in several villages of Northumberland and Durham; and Long Sword dances in the North Riding of Yorkshire.

Midland Morris Dances. At Bampton, Oxfordshire, on Whit-Monday.

Lancashire Morris Dance. At Royton, Lancashire.

Derbyshire Morris Dance. At Winster, Derbyshire, usually in July.

Coconut Dance. At Bacup, Lancashire, usually on Easter Monday.

Helston Furry Processional Dance. At Helston, Cornwall, on May 8th.

Hobby Horse Ceremonies. At Padstow, Cornwall, on May Day and at Minehead, Somerset, on the eve of May Day and on May 1st.

Horn Dance. At Abbots Bromley, Staffordshire, on the Monday following the first Sunday after September 4th (Wakes Monday).

Country Dances. In several country villages, particularly in Northumberland and Durham.

Intending spectators are advised to enquire of the English Folk Dance and Song Society before making a special journey.

The English Folk Dance and Song Society arranges Dance Parties, Festivals and Classes at Cecil Sharp House, London, and in towns and villages all over the country. For particulars apply to the Secretary, E.F.D.S.S., Cecil Sharp House, 2 Regent's Park Road, London, N.W.1.

DANCES OF WALES

BY LOÏS BLAKE

The Puritan movement of the eighteenth century did much to discourage dancing in Wales. *Rhybudd teg mewn pryd da* (A fair warning in good time) was one of many sermons aimed against mixed dancing and the playing of the harp. Yet itinerant musicians, covering long distances on little mountain ponies, were still welcome at village inn or drovers' rest. Inspired by the music, men were ever ready for a trial of skill, and, worked up into a '*hwyl*' (literally, a ship in full sail), displayed great virtuosity in jigs and clog dances. At such gatherings, seldom witnessed by the outsider, dancing over the broom-handle, or over two clay pipes laid on a sheepskin, and the squatting Toby or Kibby dance are still practised today. *Twm yn dawnsio iw gariad* (Tom dancing to his sweetheart) was danced by two people, very fast, and when one gave up another took his place.

SEASONAL CUSTOMS

Dawnsio haf (summer dancing) survived in some districts up to the 1914 war. On May Day or at Midsummer the men went out dancing in serpentine procession, waving white handkerchiefs and carrying the carefully prepared *Fedwen Haf* or *Fedwen Ifan* (the summer, or St. John's, birch). At each stopping-place they performed a number of dances, usually in columns of six. The *Cadi* (Kate), who was dressed as a woman, or in partial attire of both sexes, accompanied them. He was elected to the office, collected donations in a ladle, acted as chief marshal and, with the Fool, provided the fun of the occasion. A similar couple accompanied the *Gwassailwyr* (wassailers) who went round between Christmas and New Year carrying the *Mari Lwyd* (grey mare).

These *Gwassailwyr* sometimes danced a three-handed reel or broom dance and sometimes beat each other with staves.

COUNTRY DANCES

A three-handed reel, with twelve different figures, was danced at Llys Llanover, Monmouth, up to the death of the family harper, Thomas Gruffydd, in 1887. It was recollected and revived by his daughter and is now popular throughout Wales. A smooth Polka step is used, except where the man displays his best jig steps to each partner in turn.*

A four-handed reel and a simple long dance were collected at Port Eynon, Gower. A number of dances with Welsh associations have been found in the early dance manuals of Playford and Walsh and are being revived by *Cymdeithas Ddawns Werin Cymru* (the Welsh Folk Dance Society).

MUSIC

The polyphonic singing of the Welsh is renowned. Less well known is Penillion singing, in which the singer sets verses in original counterpoint to a traditional melody played by a harper. The harp is still the instrument of Wales, though the old triple harp is now seldom used. Many traditional dance airs, still played by the harpers, were preserved in early collections, and some—such as *Meillionen* (The clover) and *Croen y ddafad felan* (The yellow sheep-skin)—were used for dances by Walsh and Playford. The *crwth*, which differs from the viol in having the bridge set aslant, has baffled attempts at revival. The *pib-gorn* (horn pipe), once commonly made by country boys, is a seven-holed pipe, a reed in the mouth-piece and an amplifying horn at the other end.

* Three good dances are mentioned by William Jones of Llangadfan in a letter to Edward Jones, harper to George IV. A circular figure, The Round O, comes gaily between each part.

COSTUME

The women's beaver hat associated with Wales varies considerably from a wide brim in Gwent to a narrow brim and tall crown in Cardigan. A cap, worn under the hat, has four rows of frills over the ears, but does not show on the forehead. The dress consists of *pais a becwn* (petticoat and gown), the gown looped up and pinned behind, or a tight bodice with a basque. Petticoats were many, the top one often striped. Older women wore black, sometimes 'quilted almost to the heart'. Aprons might be striped, checked or plain; a neckerchief was crossed and tied behind, or tucked into an open-necked bodice; buckled shoes for best, but clogs were worn about the farms. For ceremonial dancing the men wore 'white shirts, neatly pleated, knee ties depending almost to the ankles'. Corduroy, scrubbed nearly white, was used for waistcoats and breeches; straw hats profusely decorated with ribbon for May dancing.

The travesty of Welsh costume frequently worn by small children at *Eisteddfodau* and other gatherings is as undesirable as the dressing of girls to represent men for the pseudo-folk dances with which the habit is associated. Those who still treasure the hats, dresses and other accessories of their grandparents are meticulous about every detail when, on occasion, they wear their regional costume.

WHERE DANCING MAY BE SEEN

October to May: Corwen, Merioneth. Honorary Secretary: Gwenllian Berwyn, Alwenfa, Corwen, Merioneth.

Thursday evenings: Pontypool, Monmouthshire. Miss Doris Freeman, County Education Office, Newport, Mon.

Summer dancing arranged by Cymdeithas Ddawns Werin Cymru. Honorary Secretary: Miss Daniels-Jones, County Education Office, Ruthin, Denbighshire.

THE DANCES

TECHNICAL EDITORS
MURIEL WEBSTER AND KATHLEEN P. TUCK

※※※※※※

*ABBREVIATIONS
USED IN DESCRIPTION OF STEPS AND DANCES*

r—right ⎫ referring to R—right ⎫ describing turns or
l—left ⎭ hand, foot, etc. L—left ⎭ ground pattern
C—clockwise C-C—counter-clockwise

The term 'to honour' signifies to bow or curtsey.

Reference books for description of figures:

The Country Dance Book I–VI. Cecil J. Sharp. Novello & Co., London.

The Country Dance Book, Graded Series I–XI. Cecil J. Sharp, ed. Maud Karpeles. Novello & Co.

12 Traditional Country Dances. Maud Karpeles. Published by the English Folk Dance and Song Society, London.

The Morris Book I–V. Cecil J. Sharp. Novello & Co.

The descriptions of the dances Speed the Plough and Lads a Bunchum have been adapted from Cecil Sharp's notations published in *The Country Dance Book*, Part I, and *The Morris Book*, Part II, respectively. These and the three tunes in the English selection are published by permission of Messrs. Novello & Co. The tune for Rhif Wyth is published by permission of Messrs. Stainer & Bell, from whom the 'duple' version (arranged by Arnold Foster and G. M. Griffin) may be obtained.

DANCES OF ENGLAND

POISE OF THE BODY AND HOLDS

A good carriage is of great importance. The poise of the body should be natural and easy and the weight should always be carried over the supporting foot. Unless otherwise indicated, the arms hang freely by the sides.

In ring movements or in taking both hands, the man's hands should be undermost, palms up; the woman places her hands, palms downwards, into those of the man. Shoulders and arms should be flexible, and the hands fall to a natural level.

In 'leading' partners take right hand in right, or left hand in left.

In 'swinging' (i.e. turning) partners either give both hands, right in left and left in right, or else engage Valse fashion. The former is the older method.

BASIC STEPS

The choice of steps in the Country Dances is not strictly prescribed. They include the following: running, walking, skipping, slipping, Polka, change-hop, and pivot.

The first five steps need no explanation. The change-hop is similar to the Polka but in even rhythm and less accented. In the pivot step, dancers step on to right foot, keeping weight well over the foot; push off with the ball of the left foot, at the same time lifting right foot slightly to replace it in the direction in which the movement is being made.

The steps are performed on the ball of the foot and always with a lilt, or—as a traditional dancer put it—'not so much with the legs as with the hitch-up of the body'. The steps should be neatly performed and with economy of movement: e.g. the knees are not raised nor the toes pointed. The general style of the Country Dance is its 'gay simplicity'.

Partners always honour each other at the conclusion of the dance (i.e. on the 3rd beat of the last bar). The man bows and the woman usually makes a slight curtsey or bob.

SPEED THE PLOUGH

Country Dance

Region   Noted in Surrey, but not peculiar to any particular region.

Character   Gay, but dignified.

Formation   Longways for as many as will. Partners face each other in 2 parallel lines, men with l and women with r shoulders to the front. The figures are performed simultaneously by groups of 2 adjacent couples ($\square$ = man, $\bigcirc$ = woman).

```
              2   1   2   1
       DOWN   □   □   □   □   UP
              O   O   O   O
              2   1   2   1
```

Dance | MUSIC
Except for the 2nd half of Figure II and Figure IV, a walking step is recommended. | *Bars*

FIGURE I: VISITING	A(1)
1st man leads his partner down to visit 2nd woman. On the 1st beat of the 3rd bar they 'honour' her, she responding; the 1st couple then falls back a little way.	1–4
1st couple visits 2nd man in like manner.	5–8
FIGURE II: DOWN THE MIDDLE AND BACK	A(2)
1st man leads his partner down the middle of the Set.	1–4
They face and, taking both hands, slip up to places.	5–8
FIGURE III: CROSS OVER	B(1)
Partners cross over l shoulders into each other's places and make a half-turn C.	1–4
Partners return to places, passing r shoulders and making a half-turn C-C.	5–8
FIGURE IV: SWING AND CHANGE	B(2)
Partners swing, turning C, and at the same time the two couples change places, moving round each other in a C direction (change-hop step).	1–8

The above figures are repeated ad lib., but each time with a new combination of couples. The 1st couples will have moved down one place in the Set and so will dance with the new couples immediately below them, whilst the 2nd couples, who have moved up, will dance with the couples immediately above them. On reaching the top or the bottom of the Set, dancers remain inactive for one round of figures and then continue to dance in the reverse direction; i.e. the 1st couples become 2nd couples and vice versa.

SPEED THE PLOUGH

Collected by Cecil Sharp
Arranged by Arnold Foster

CIRCASSIAN CIRCLE

Country Dance to the tune of 'Haste to the Wedding'

Region — Noted in Northumberland, but not peculiar to any particular region.

Character — Lively.

Formation — Round for as many as will. Dancers stand in a circle, facing centre, each man with his partner on his R.

Dance	MUSIC *Bars*
FIGURE I: ALL TO THE CENTRE All take hands and dance forward and back (running step). Repeat.	A(1) 1–4 5–8
FIGURE II: WOMEN AND MEN TO CENTRE Women dance forward to the centre, bowing on the 2nd beat of the 2nd bar, and back to places. Men dance forward, bowing on 2nd beat of bar 6. Men face their contrary partners (i.e. the women on their L) and dance towards them.	A(2) 1–4 5–8
FIGURE III: SWING Men swing their contrary partners, turning C, either taking both hands (skipping step) or else engaging *Valse* fashion (pivot step).	B(1) 1–8

CIRCASSIAN CIRCLE
Tune: *Haste to the Wedding*

Collected by Cecil Sharp
Arranged by Arnold Foster

FIGURE IV: PROMENADE Each man places his r arm round the waist of his new partner and all dance round C-C, one couple behind another, men on the inside (skipping step). The above figures are repeated as often as desired, the men dancing with a new partner in each repetition.	B(2) 1–8

LADS A BUNCHUM

Morris Dance

Region   Adderbury, Oxfordshire.

Character   Vigorous and ceremonial.

Formation   Six men standing in two parallel lines facing up. The dancers wear bells on their legs (see p. 11).

```
              5   3   1
              □   □   □
      DOWN    □   □   □    UP
              6   4   2
```

Each dancer carries a wooden stick 33 inches long and 1 inch in diameter. Throughout the A music movements,

Plate 3   Maypole: costumes of c. 1840

the sticks are held in the middle in the r hand and are carried vertically, well in front of the body, hand about shoulder level. On the 3rd beat of the last bar, partners always strike the tips (i.e. the upper half) of their sticks together.

In the B music movements, dancers perform the special stick movements described below. The beats on which the sticks are struck are marked thus in the music: ×.

DOUBLE CLAP

Each dancer holds his stick with both hands, the l hand grasping the stick about 4 inches from the lower end; the r hand, palm upward, grasps the stick about 11 inches from the tip. Preparatory to striking, the sticks are held a little in front of the body, at breast-level, and inclined slightly forward towards the R, thus:—

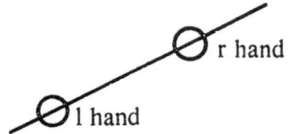

Partners face each other and tap sticks in the following way:—	MUSIC Bars
Each odd number, without releasing either hand, strikes with the tip of his stick the butt of his partner's stick (i.e. the part which lies between his two hands). Simultaneously, each even number moves his l hand slightly forward so that the butt may meet the tip of his partner's stick. This is done on the first 3 beats of the bar.	B 1
Repeat, but even numbers striking odd.	2
Odd numbers strike even [beat 1]. Even numbers strike odd [beat 2]. Repeat on beats 3 and 4.	3

Odd numbers strike even [beat 1]. Even numbers strike odd [beat 2]. Partners strike the tips of their sticks together, moving them from R to L [beat 3].	4
Repeat movements as in bars 1–4.	5–8

SINGLE CLAP

Same as in Double Clap, except that sticks are held in the middle by the r hand only.

CLAP HIGH

Partners, holding their sticks in both hands, as in Double Clap, turn l shoulders to each other and raise their sticks well above their heads. Even numbers hold sticks horizontally and parallel with the files. Odd numbers strike partner's sticks, each dancer making an overhand movement, r over l, so as to strike down with his tip upon his partner's butt. Strike three times as in Double Clap.	1
Movement is reversed, even numbers striking partner's sticks which are held horizontally.	2
Partners face each other and strike as in Double Clap.	3–4
Repeat movements of bars 1–4.	5–8

Steps

In all A music movements, except Once-to-yourself, the following Morris step sequence is used (hr=hop right; hl= hop left; ft=feet together).

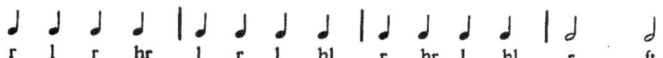

The change of foot, as well as the hop, is made with a slight spring, i.e. the weight of the body is raised from the ground before each step, so that the change of foot takes place in the air. The dancer alights on the ball of the foot with the supporting leg held straight under the body. At the same time, the free leg is swung forward from the hip, the lower leg hanging loosely from the knee. The free leg remains in this position until the next change of foot. It is then swung sharply back and the foot takes the ground under the body.

Dance	MUSIC *Bars*
FIGURE I: ONCE-TO-YOURSELF Dancers walk round in a ring C to places (2 steps to the bar) and finish in two lines facing partners.	Introduction
FIGURE II: FOOT-UP Dancers, facing up, move forward and back. Repeat as in bars 1–4.	A 1–4 5–8
FIGURE III: DOUBLE CLAP	B 1–8
FIGURE IV: BACK-TO-BACK Partners face, move forward, passing r shoulders and move round each other back to places, facing always in the same direction. Repeat as in bars 1–4 but passing l shoulders.	A 1–4 5–8
FIGURE V: SINGLE CLAP	B 1–8
FIGURE VI: PROCESSIONAL-DOWN Partners face, except Nos. 1 and 2, who dance down between Nos. 3 and 4 and back to places. Nos. 3 and 4, followed by Nos. 1 and 2, dance down between Nos. 5 and 6 and back to places.	A 1–4 5–8
FIGURE VII: CLAP HIGH	B 1–8

LADS A BUNCHUM

Collected by Cecil Sharp
Arranged by Arnold Foster

Play 6 times

FIGURE VIII: PROCESSIONAL-UP
Partners face, except Nos. 5 and 6, who dance up between Nos. 3 and 4 and back to places.
Nos. 3 and 4, followed by Nos. 5 and 6, dance up between Nos. 1 and 2 and back to places.

A
1–4

5–8

FIGURE IX: DOUBLE CLAP

B
1–8

FIGURE X: DANCE-ROUND
Partners clasp r hands, shoulders level, arms straight, and dance round C to places. Meanwhile the stick is held in the l hand with outstretched arm, and is shifted into the r hand in time to tap sticks in the last bar.
Repeat, clasping l hands and dancing round C-C.

A
1–4

5–8

FIGURE XI: SINGLE CLAP

B
1–8

FIGURE XII: WHOLE-HEY (FIGURE OF EIGHT)

A

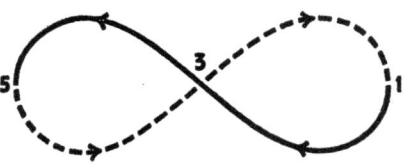

Nos. 1, 3, 5 describe the figure of eight, as shown in the above diagram, passing along the unbroken line as they move down the Set and along the dotted line as they move up. Nos. 2, 4, 6 perform the same figure simultaneously.

1–8

FIGURE XIII: CLAP HIGH
Dancers face up as they make the final stick tap.

B
1–8

A WELSH DANCE

RHIF WYTH (*Figure of Eight*)

Region Llanover, Monmouthshire.

Character Smooth, neat Polka step. All the dancers step on the spot, with a heel and toe jig, in the last bar of Figures 1, 2, 3, 4 and 8.

Formation Longways, partners facing each other. Progressive triple minor set, for any number; but, since the 3rd couples are completely inactive, they are generally omitted, the 1st couples dancing Figures 2 and 3 round the next 2nd couples.

Dance	MUSIC Bars
1 1st couple move down outside the 2nd couple, meet and turn with right hands (elbows bent).	A 1–8
2 Repeat below next couple.	1–8
3 1st couple cross over passing right, move up outside one couple and dance half a figure of eight through that couple.	B(1) 1–8
4 Repeat the movement round the next couple, finishing in original places.	B(2) 1–8
5 1st couple make ring with 2nd woman, twice round, C.	A 1–8
6 Repeat with 2nd man.	1–8

RHIF WYTH

7 1st couple dance the Hey with 2nd woman, who passes right with 1st man.	B(1) 1–8
8 Repeat with 2nd man, who passes right with 1st woman. 1st couple cast down to 2nd place.	B(2) 1–8
In Figures 5 to 8 the movement of the 1st couple is continuous.	

BIBLIOGRAPHY

ENGLAND

ALFORD, VIOLET.—'Morris and Moresca.' *Journal of the E.F.D.S.S.*, 1935.
—— 'Some Hobby Horses of Great Britain.' *Ib.*, 1939.
—— 'The Maypole.' *Ib.*, 1943.
—— and GALLOP, RODNEY.—*The Traditional Dance*. London, 1935.
CHAMBERS, SIR E. K.—*The English Folk Play*. Oxford, 1933.
FOX STRANGWAYS, A. H., and KARPELES, MAUD.—*Cecil Sharp*. Oxford, 1933.
GALLOP, RODNEY.—'The Origins of the Morris Dance.' *Journal of the E.F.D.S.S.*, 1934.
KARPELES, MAUD.—'English Folk Dances, their Survival and Revival.' *Folk-Lore*, vol. XLIII, 1932.
—— *12 Traditional Dances*. London, 1931.
—— *The Lancashire Morris Dance; Lancashire Morris Dance Tunes*. London, 1930.
KENNEDY, D. N.—*England's Dances*. London, 1949.
—— 'Dramatic Elements in the Folk Dance.' *Journal of the E.F.D.S.S.*, 1949.

Plate 4
Welshwomen's dress of c. 1850

KIDSON, F., and NEAL, MARY.—*English Folk Song and Dance*. Cambridge 1915.
NEEDHAM, JOSEPH.—'The Geographical Distribution of English Ceremonial Dance.' *Journal of the E.F.D.S.S.*, 1936.
SHARP, CECIL J.—*The Morris Book*, Parts 1-5; *Morris Dance Tunes*, Sets 1-11. (Tunes and descriptions of 95 dances.) London, 1907-24.
—— *The Sword Dances of Northern England*, Parts 1-3; *Sword Dance Tunes*, Sets 1-3. (Tunes and descriptions of 16 dances.) London, 1911-13.
—— *The Country Dance Book*, Parts 1-6; *Country Dance Tunes*, Sets 1-11. (Tunes and descriptions of 177 dances.) London, 1909-27.
—— (ed. Maud Karpeles).—*The Country Dance: Graded Series*, Sets 1-9. (Tunes and descriptions of 54 dances.) London, 1926-34.

And other publications and reprints issued by Novello & Co., and the English Folk Dance and Song Society. Many gramophone records are obtainable from the Sales Department at Cecil Sharp House and at the Gramophone Company's dealers.

WALES

BLAKE, Loïs.—*Meillionen*. Gwynn Publishing Co., Llangollen, 1949.
—— *Welsh Folk Dance: a Survey*. Gwynn Publishing Co., Llangollen, 1948.
—— *The Welsh Whim and other Dances*. Gwynn Publishing Co., Llangollen, 1947.
—— *The Welsh Morris and other Dances*. Gwynn Publishing Co., Llangollen, 1939.
—— *The Llangadfan Dances*. Hughes & Son, Cardiff, 1936.
GRIFFIN, GLADYS.—*Rhif Wyth*. Stainer & Bell, London.
—— *The Welsh Reel*. Stainer & Bell, London.
GWYNN WILLIAMS, W. S.—*Welsh National Music and Dance*. Hughes & Son, Cardiff, 1932.
—— *Cadi Ha, Song and Dance*. Gwynn Publishing Co., Llangollen.
Journal of the Welsh Folk Song Society, 1912-48.

GRAMOPHONE RECORDS.—The Welsh Reel and Rhif Wyth: Columbia D.B. 1623.
The Gower Reel: Columbia F.B. 1570.

www.ingramcontent.com/pod-product-compliance
Lightning Source LLC
Chambersburg PA
CBHW061743290426
43661CB00127B/966